Networking for Business

Contacts +
Opportunity =
Success

It's not just who you know, it's what you do once you know them!

Lessons from Serial Entrepreneur
Guy T, Dunn Sr.

ISBN-13: 978-1470163792
ISBN-10: 1470163799

This book was compiled by my daughter *Courtney Dunn* and *Sandra Myers*, and edited by *Robin Coffman, Joyce Chester* and *A.L. Layacan*.

I appreciate them for helping me to get this out on paper and allowing me to express myself.

The forward was written by Terence Ferrell.

Terence has become a good friend and I appreciate him wanting to help with my book as well as the kind words he said about me.

Jay Osterholm was a contributor to my book. He helped frame it so it had a larger appeal and just gave it more substance . I appreciate him more than he will ever know.

I dedicate this book to my parents who have always encouraged my outgoing personality.

I further dedicate this to my wife and best friend, Judi, who has put up with my being out networking all the time and makes home the place I always want to be at the end of the day.

<u>Other Books By or Featuring Guy T. Dunn Sr.</u>
Maybe You Can Do It Yourself – Quick Computer Fixes for the Non Geek
(www.maybeyoucandoityourself.com)

A Cup of Cappuccino for the Entrepreneur's Spirit Volume II

Both are available on Amazon.com

Schedule Guy to Speak at your Event
215-680-9192

Guy is your ideal speaker for:
- Conference Keynotes
- Conference Workshops
- Leadership Retreats
- Networking Events
- Sales Team Meetings

<u>Top Topics</u>
How Proper Networking Never Fails To Grow Your Business.

Networking And Technology – A Marriage Made In Heaven

Brand Yourself With A Newsletter

Empower and Equip Others!
Share this Book

Networking For Business
Contacts + Opportunity = Success

It's not just who you know, It's what you do once you know them!

Wouldn't it be great to have a manual to help you understand and execute your networking activities. One that lays it out so you develop a plan to win every time? Give your networking activities a boost. Make sure you are armed with the knowledge to make every event count. These tips and stories are easy to read, understand and implement. So share it with network!

Special Quantity Discounts

2-20	Books	$ 8.50
21-99	Books	$7.50
100-499	Books	$7.00
500 +	Books	$6.00

To Place Order Call 215-680-9192

Table of Contents

Foreword

by Terence Farrell

Networking is a key to success in business and politics. This is particularly true for the small business person, who must make every advertising dollar and effort count. In politics, my profession, getting to meet people and having them get to know and like you - and ultimately to vote for you - is the lifeblood of success.

In this, his second book, Guy T. Dunn Sr. , writes passionately and informatively about what he knows well: networking and its positive impact on business and life. An experienced and consummate networker, he knows of what he speaks, and this quick- read of a book contains many useful tips both for those beginning to network and those with years under their belts.

It was in a networking context that I first met Guy Dunn, back in 2007, when I ran for my first term as County Commissioner, and was told by professional consultants that if I truly wanted to win what shaped up to be a challenging race, I needed to be "everywhere, all the time." I happened to go to a seminar then, not so much for whatever knowledge was being offered - I forget now what the topic was - but as always, primarily to meet people. Like me, Guy was one of the few African Americans in the room. Naturally, we met afterwards, exchanged names, conversation and cards. That was the start of what has grown to be a good friendship.

What impressed me most about Guy, in addition to his infectious smile and out-going personality, were his professionalism and follow-through over the next several weeks (and ultimately years!). He sent me an email the next day, put me on his newsletter list, remembered my name at the next event, stayed in constant, though not overwhelming, contact. Amazingly, I began to see him everywhere I campaigned - from Chamber of Commerce breakfast meetings, to evening events for non-profit organizations, to offbeat events where I thought I would see no familiar face - there was Guy Dunn!

This book is, at its core, an examination and analysis of the many tools and strategies available for networking in our modern, Internet world - e.g., email newsletters, websites, and social media - to achieve business success. It is also, perhaps more importantly, about creating success in one's personal life. I found the book's next to last chapter [Success and all its Meanings] particularly intriguing. It's not all about the money! A successful life is a balancing act - between work and play, between seeking "strategic alliances" (a concept explored in a chapter) and relaxing at home with your family.

As an elected official, I struggle with achieving this balance. We Commissioners (three of us form the governing body for the County) could wear ourselves ragged trying to attend even most, if not all, of the speaking opportunities, fundraisers, and other events to which we are invited. As difficult as it is, sometimes we just have to say "no," stay home, and enjoy being with loved ones.

This balance is a goal Mr. Dunn has achieved. He makes that clear in the book's dedication, in part to his "wife and best friend, Judi, who has put up with my being out networking all the time and makes home the place I always want to be at the end of the day."

In the final analysis, the true benefit of this well-thought-out book, is not only the knowledge and know-how conveyed to build one's business success as Guy has done with his Geeks on Call franchises, but it is also the motivation and inspiration to keep going through difficult times, climbing that mountain called success, ever growing in business and life. You may never achieve the 11,000 first-generation LinkedIn connections that Mr. Dunn has, but being inspired by and applying the networking tips from this little gem of a book, your business and life can be better tomorrow than it is today.

Enjoy, learn, and keep on keeping on!

Terence Farrell, first elected as a Commissioner in 2007 and re-elected overwhelmingly in 2011, currently serves as chairman of the board of Chester County Commissioners.

Introduction

We each have a voice—whether it is to sing, to teach, to motivate, to inspire, or to help others. Personally, I have always been able to see things in a positive way. I don't let much get me down or upset, so my voice is my ability to help people see things positively. Now I may not be able to change a pessimist to an optimist and I wouldn't even try. What I will do is show the pessimist that the other side of the coin—the optimistic side—is just as valid.

I heard an interview with Maya Angelou today on the radio. What she said resonated in me; it's exactly how I think. She referred to the quote: As you ramble on through life brother, whatever be your goal, keep your eye upon the doughnut and not upon the hole. I have been able to help people make the decision to be better—to stay focused on the donut. I help people keep trying, even when they think it is fruitless. My 'voice' is to encourage them to go through it and then come out stronger because what some see as an insurmountable mountain, I see as a hill to climb, knowing there is something better on the other side.

So have a donut on me and leave the holes!

My name is Guy Dunn. In 2006, I bought a 'Geeks on Call' computer franchise after a two-year stint as a director of business development with a systems engineering firm. In that role, I would travel all over the country securing government contracts and marketing to large government contractors. I enjoyed these interactions, as I am a very social person.

Another aspect of my job was researching businesses that our company might take-over. While scouting out IT firms for our company to acquire, a Geeks on Call business opportunity came across my radar screen. I checked it out; three territories were for sale because the owner was sick and unable to maintain the business. There were a few issues, but overall it seemed like a sound investment. The franchise organization was solid and had a good reputation. When I brought the opportunity to my company's owner, he passed on it. By then I had researched it enough that I was itching to go for it, so I made the decision to buy the business myself.

You see I was no stranger to business. I had grown up in a family business and had started, grown and sold a multimillion dollar business. I had been a CFO, a business management consultant and a trader of gold, diamonds and computers internationally. I was and still am a serial entrepreneur in my own right. Who I am is all about being in business. This was just going to be my next chapter.

The Geeks on Call franchise that I bought included geographic territories that I would also be acquiring. These territories were in areas in which, I had no relationships at all. They covered the Southern and Western Philadelphia suburbs. Most of my business life had been in the city of Philadelphia, so having to develop a computer business in an unfamiliar area was going to be a challenge. The thing about me is that a challenge is just another way to say an adventure. A new mountain to climb and conquer.

If you didn't notice, I did not mention any professional experience in computer repairs at any time in my career. That's because there was none. I was never trained in computer repairs; computers were a hobby of mine. I taught myself how to fix them and I would take them apart and put them back together for fun. I actually had a room of computers in various levels of assembly when I was living alone in my apartment. I was, of course, the go-to-guy for family and friends when it came to computer issues.

When I researched this franchise opportunity, I decided to take my hobby and make money doing it. You can't ask for anything better. When you can make money doing what you love to do, you are a winner!

So now I had my business and a few customers due to franchise advertising and reputation. If I wanted to succeed, however, I would have to get new customers and grow this business. Since it was in an area that I did not have contacts in, I had to figure out a way to get my name out and build my business. I went back to what I had done most of my life in business—networking.

Networking comes naturally to me. I love meeting new people and I try to develop relationships by trying to find ways to help the people I meet. I think the best way to get people to get to know you is by finding a way to assist them. They will always appreciate unsolicited help. Many people find it stressful and intimidating to go to networking events where they do not know the people there. I like the challenge of developing new relationships and finding ways to work with new people.

I found a new piece of the puzzle a little later. In one of the groups that I joined while networking, a women was publishing a monthly newsletter of networking events. I was using this to schedule my monthly calendar to be sure to get to these events. I loved that newsletter. However, it only covered a small portion of the territories where my business was located. Her useful newsletter gave me the idea to make my own newsletter doing the same thing, just expand it to include the additional areas I covered. Me being the impulsive person that I am, I decided that was what I would do and subscribed to Constant Contact. My newsletter was born. In these pages you will see how I used this newsletter and networking to make contacts and build my business.

This book is a compilation of some of my strategies on staying optimistic, networking, and using tools (like a newsletter) to strengthen your business. I think these ideas will resonate with many people. Hopefully it can help to motivate you, inspire you and get you to think about ways that you can do more with your business and in your lives.

I still publish my newsletter and it has evolved into a website. If you are interested, it can be found at www.theideaguyonline.com. I also publish a monthly magazine and have other book projects coming out. Access to all of my different projects is available through my website. And some of my success has even been showcased in an article on the cover of the Philadelphia Business Journal, Published June 5th, 2009.

A New Year Means a Fresh Start

A New Year is here! With a fresh new year, we can take this time to set goals and make our lives better. Many of us promise ourselves we will lose weight, quit smoking, eat healthy, be more organized, etc. It is interesting that we wait on the calendar before we will decide to make a change for the better. Why wait?

My wish for us all, as we head into this new year, is that we try to be better every day. We don't need to wait for a date on the calendar to decide to be better. If we decide that we only want to be better by just a little each day, say 1%, by this time next year, we will be 365% better than we are now. Can you imagine being 365 percent better than you are now? How awesome would that be? Little steps add up over time!

Look at this, not as the start of a new year, but a start to a new way of life. To help yourself move forward, make notes in a notebook or journal about your improvements each day. If, on some days, you feel you didn't meet that 1% improvement mark, don't be hard on yourself. Allow for occasional missteps - tomorrow is another day. Trying to move forward is all you can ask of yourself.

Since this is a new year, it may be a good time to stretch yourself a little and grow your business in the process. (1) Volunteer your time and broaden your network while helping others. (2) Talk to people about your business at every opportunity and stress how your business can help them or their business. (3) Commit to a greater number of contacts each month. Chose a number that is larger than last year's.

Taking advantage of current events like elections, charity runs, and similar causes can not only help you participate in a cause you believe in, but help you to build new relationships. An upcoming election can present wonderful opportunities for you to network with people who you know and many who you do not know.

Top 5 things to remember about a Fresh Start

1. You can start something new any day of the year. Don't wait, do it now.
2. Small steps every day leads to big gains over time.
3. You have to allow for a misstep now and then, but don't dwell on it. Acknowledge it and get back on track.
4. Stretch yourself; reach higher and commit to do a little more than before.
5. You make opportunities by being a part of something, so find a cause and use it to expand

your network while feeling good about what you believe it.

Set Yourself up for "Luck"

Being in the right place at the right time can change your life. There are times we can get lucky and meet someone that impacts our life, like a customer with a big deal. Those are rare occasions but they do happen. There are ways to make those types of things happen more often.

Talking to the people around you means that you are networking and finding people that may be interested in hearing what you have to say. If you are sitting in a deli or a coffee shop, how are those around you going to know you have something they may be interested in if you don't tell them?

When success happens, you will probably tell someone later that you just happened to run into someone that was interested in networking with you and it changed your life. Give yourself some credit. You were the one that initiated the conversation. You approached that person. You put yourself in the right place when luck just happened.

Putting yourself in the right places leads to opportunities for things to happen in your life. Many times, the impression of being at the right place at the right time can be made to happen, when you work at it.

If you are looking for a break, do you think that break will happen while you are sitting at home watching sitcoms or by going to a play or the premier of a movie? You have to let people know what you want to happen in your life and then find people to help you make it happen. A great way to do that is to ask for help.

Don't be afraid or embarrassed to ask someone if they could give you some advice. Most people are flattered that you asked and will give you all the advice you want. When others know you are working to get ahead, they are willing to help you make connections or reach those that need your product. Most are more willing to help if they know you will reciprocate with your skills.

Make it a point to regularly ask yourself where you will be in six months or five years. If you see yourself as an architect, go to an architectural convention. If you want to be a musician, go to workshops on how to be a musician or places to be exposed to music and musicians. Try out for American Idol, go to open calls for talent.

If you want to sell products or services to businesses, join one or more of your local chambers, like the Chamber of Commerce. Find out when the meeting dates are by looking in the local newspaper or online and attend their meetings. You will find yourself connecting with people who will influence your life.

Lastly, "fake it until you make it." What I mean is, sometimes you have to look the part if you want to get the part. Having confidence that you belong is part of the battle. Like in the movie with Michael J. Fox, The Secret of My Success, sometimes, you have to act like the person you want to be so people will take you seriously.

Now, don't take it to his extreme. I just want you to walk the walk and talk the talk so people will look at you as if you already are one of them, not someone who is trying to be one of them. Most people are unable to imagine how someone or something would look if dressed or decorated differently. You have to show them.

You can set yourself up for a "lucky break" by frequenting a place where you are more apt to find opportunities. Find ways to be in the right place at the right time. Look for events, organizations, people who can help you reach your goals. Look for ways to be around people who are who you want to be, have what you want to have, and/or need what you have to sell. Dress like the person you want to be. Your appearance will determine your first impression and you only get one first impression.

I am writing much of this while on vacation in Florida and it seems like a great segue (pronounced seg-way) to how we should not minimize the power of networking wherever we are. One thing is that you never know who you will meet and how they can help you, or better yet, how you can help them. I believe that everything happens for a reason. There are no coincidences. I believe people are put in your lives when they should be. It is up to us to be open to the opportunities life throws at us. That said, you have to continually put yourself in the path of opportunity.

Talk to that person at the bar next to you. He may be just the person you need to launch your product. Chat up the person next to you on the deck of the cruise ship or in the seat next to you on the plane. He may know someone at the company you are trying to get in touch with. Don't be afraid to open up and be friendly wherever you go. Be open to opportunities.

Look for opportunities to help others. You can't go wrong spreading good karma. If you meet someone and have an opportunity to help, do it. As Nike's slogan reminds us, don't think about it, "Just do it." Life is about how we can help each other. If everyone did this, the world would be a better place. I trust that if you give, the world will give back. I believe that there are many of you who feel the same way. So while you are sipping that Pina Colada, talk to someone and tell your story. You never know, they may be in your next chapter.

Top 5 Things to Remember about Luck

1. Luck rarely happens if you don't set it up. Help luck to find you by being at places you want your life to go.
2. You can get more lucky breaks by looking the part.
3. Luck is sometimes opportunity in disguise. Look around because there are always opportunities to be lucky.
4. Luck can happen at any time, with anyone. Talk to people you come across during your daily travels, you never know.
5. Luck sometimes is the universes reward for good deeds. Help people and you may help luck to find you.

Grow your Business By Branding Yourself

To be successful in business, you need to learn from the best, adapt that knowledge to your style and implement your own ideas and skills. This process of going beyond the comfortable norm has been clichéd as 'thinking outside of the box.' While many cat-owners may not want their pets thinking outside the 'box', in order to grow your business you must always push beyond others and find clear points of differentiation.

My newsletter is a tactical example of me getting out of the box (of normal and comfortable) to market my business. As I mentioned in my introduction, a woman I know was doing a listing of events for the Women's Referral Network of Chester County. I have to admit that I borrowed this idea from her because I saw the value in it as a tool to get information out to people. I also saw that it was a great way for me to stay in front of people month after month. So, I emulated her listing, but expanded it to include geographic areas she did not cover.

Newsletters can contain a wealth of information that you can use in expanding your business contacts. If you can't find a newsletter directed toward your business, create your own. Approach others for advertising and articles. It will open up ways to expand your networking contacts. Ask people if they would appreciate receiving your newsletter. Most of them will see the value when they hear what you intend to put in your newsletter.

The most important functions of a newsletter are to: 1) document and share your opinion / point of view, 2) build credibility, 3) build a following and 4) build a dialogue. A newsletter is means of sharing information and staying relevant without being intrusive. Look at how others have designed their newsletters; understand your audience and then build a letter that you feel represents you. Sharing and commenting on industry related news is a great way of providing timely and relevant information.

The big difference between my newsletter and the other one was that I added a monthly blog of my thoughts and I would find a good networking article on the internet and add it to my newsletter. This addition set mine apart. The purpose of the newsletter was to brand me as the go-to guy for networking as well as to keep me and my business in front of people every month.

I still go to a lot of networking events and I add anyone's business card I got to my list, which has grown. I always get positive comments about my newsletter and try to make sure it has quality and relevant content. Now, I am spending four or six hours a month gathering this information, putting it together and getting it out for all to read.

You may ask, how does this help me? I print my newsletter for the exposure. People all over the Philadelphia area know me because of my newsletter. When I come into a room at a networking event, I know many of the people there simply because I have positioned myself as the "networking guy." It is not uncommon for people who introduce me to their friends and colleagues to say, "You have to get on Guy's newsletter."

My newsletter gives me a reason to talk to people other than just about what I do. I can legitimately go up to anyone, start with the newsletter, and then go into what I do. It also helps build my business and referrals.

I believe creating new personal brands, such as a newsletter, gives you exposure in a greater way and helps to grow your business. It opens up the possibility of getting outside of just the computer business and still having a presence in this area with my newsletter. What way can you do something outside of the box to grow your business?

After meeting with people personally for years to distribute my newsletter, I have evolved it into a different format. I have made my newsletter into a website. This opens the door for more creativity and more opportunities to expand—to be a greater resource for everyone as a well as a place for people to advertise and reach a captive audience.

Key Takeaways

1. Building lasting connections, means staying visible and relevant to your contacts
2. Newsletters are great tactics
3. The most important functions of a newsletter are to: 1) document and share your opinion / point of view, 2) build credibility, 3) build a following and 4) build a dialogue
4. In building connections, you are building your personal brand – this is what people will remember and identify as you.

How Does YOUR Business Grow?

Metrics, metrics and more metrics. From the getting the first parking spot, to 'matching-out' how many business cards you must collect at that cocktail party, we setup bench-marks to measure our daily performance. But I would suggest you think about benchmarks as a war-plan, battle strategy, or rules of engagement. Military strategist all over of the World, have for countless centuries, perfected that art of battle. They think big-picture, not small unconnected engagements or actions. Growing a business is little different from a well-conceived battle plan. There are environmental conditions (economy / trends), supply lines (inventory or cash), logistics (timelines /due-dates), soldiers (you / team), and the mission (goal), the enemy (competition), alliances (enemy of my enemy) – all of which have practical correlations. Most of all, every successful battle plan is based on realistic expectations of using what you have. If you want to use something you don't have, you are going to have to somehow buy, acquire or otherwise take it away from someone else.

Everything you need to know about business can be found in the journals of great military leaders. Through both success and failure, military strategies on how to acquire, secure and over-come obstacles are often over looked by business people, as many sweat making that 'all-important' business call or follow-up on that big contact you made at the industry event of the year. Take a look at Sun Tzu's the Art of War. In the highly disciplined business culture of Japan, many businesses make this required reading for their executives.

"Opportunities multiply as they are seized."
~ Sun Tzu

"Know yourself and you will win all battles."
~ Sun Tzu

"You have to believe in yourself."
~ Sun Tzu

There is little room for feeling self-pity for setbacks. True to Sun Tzu, feelings are not considered strength, but inferred as an indulgence. So, how do we as people who are now conditioned to find our feelings compete with those who appear to be devoid of them? That's simple – there is a time and a place for almost everything. Feelings are a significant strength, but not a weapon.

It's easy to be discouraged when business is slow. People may not be coming in or calling. Every once in a while, we come to that slow period when we ask ourselves, "is this all worth it?" I have come close to looking in the want ads and/or going to Monster.com to see what is out there. What usually happens just before I do, however, is a customer calls and I end up with a big project and things start to pick up again.

This is both good and bad. The good is obviously that my business stays afloat and I am able to keep moving forward. The bad is that I let my pipeline get weak. That is the cardinal sin of being in business. Business depends on keeping your prospecting and marketing up at all times. We are letting luck and possibilities replace what should be patterned and measured results based on a consistent plan of activities. We all know marketing is based on numbers.

How many people must I reach?

How many people must I see?

How many people must I give proposals to?

How many sales must I have to be profitable?

Once we have a handle on the numbers, we have to work the math forwards and backwards, constantly modifying it to make sure we keep the pipeline and sales up.

All this goes back to your network. Have you decided how many events you need to attend each month? How many people are you targeting at each networking event?

The goal of networking is to meet people who are either prospects, now or later, a possible referral source or people you can help. This moves you closer to finding a prospect or a referral source.

We should all renew our commitment to work towards controlling how our businesses are growing by knowing the numbers and working to increase them. This is the only way we can keep ahead of the game. We should not be subject to what could happen, but be more in control of what can and will happen, if we are consistent and diligent.

I am energized and encouraged about what lies ahead. I see a future that is successful, because I have taken control of what determines success—by my efforts! Plan, implement, measure then modify and once done, do it again and again.

What is your plan for the coming year? Many of us are not doing what we did last year at this time. So what do we do? Let's talk about partnering.

Top 5 Growth Considerations

1. Learn how to build your battle-plan
2. Plan for big-picture strategies, rather than randomly or impulsively hitting targets

3. Utilize what is right in front of you rather than wasting precious energy wishing for what you don't have.
4. Use your feelings as motivation, not a strategic weapon.
5. Rely on your battle plan when all else seems bleak

Keep Moving Forward

Last year may have been a bad year for business. Mine was okay, but still not up to post-recession levels and I am not happy with that. I am tired of this recession and I am not taking it anymore. I think we should all go on strike against this recession and not participate. That being said, here is what I pledge to do while I'm on strike:

I will do at least the same amount of business as I did prior to this recession.

I will add new business each week to increase my customer list.

I will not let the economy affect my business or my attitude.

I will work my network and ask for business.

I will provide exceptional service to each and every customer.

At the same time that I am committed to these things, I am also making myself more visible and accessible to my clients. I think that being available and attentive to my clients' needs is the key to success. More importantly, it is necessary to keep in contact with clients as often as possible—without being annoying and looking like you are begging for their business. That is not always easy to do and can be very hard to gauge.

I am one who believes that we can shape our future by changing what we do today. Let's decide that this year will be the best year we can have. Let's look at our own weaknesses and shortcomings. Find that one thing that you know you can do better and do it. If you need help, ask for it. I am going to work with someone this year to help me organize my administrative efforts. You decide where you need to improve. So in the spirit of the 1960's protests, I reject the recession and call for a strike!

Overcoming Setbacks

Do you ever feel like you are sleep walking? Do you feel that you are just moving through space and not changing anything around you? I get that way sometimes. It's not always easy to keep moving forward, especially when I experience setbacks.

So what do you do? The best thing to do is to "Wake Up!" Come out of the daze and get back to the reality of your situation. Next is to identify what is not working and change it. Sometimes a small change will make a big difference. Lastly, get help. Open up to someone. Talk to someone who you trust and let them help you work through whatever you are going through. Sometimes just talking to someone will help get you back on the right track.

It's important to remember that perceptions can be relative and vary from person to person. Your perspective is shaped by perceptions. You may perceive that you have reached a major milestone and others may perceive failure. If you win a big account, but it could be a money loser – is that then a business victory? Keeping positive is all about managing your own expectations. If your goals are not realistic, then you will likely perceive you are failing or missing your target goals. Take your perceptions and continually test them against the context of external factors, things you can't control and changing landscapes.

Set-backs may or may not be as bad as you think. When things really hit-the-fan, I am usually the first to say, that it can always get worse. That doesn't make me a doom-sayer. In fact, I am an optimist. What I internalize is any positive that can be gleaned from situation; even if that is only to say – 'it could be worse.' Always look for the positives in any situation. Maybe in the end you learned something

What does this have to do with networking? When we get to feel this way we can easily become sidetracked and stop doing the things we know will move us forward, like networking. We withdraw and stop reaching out because of the fog we are in. Sometimes I take time off when I just want to vegetate and watch a movie or TV show without the distraction of my business interests. We all need time to rest and regroup. Renew your efforts and you will see that it does work, if you keep on plugging.

Once you have regrouped, it is time to get back at it. There is a saying that I love: "you've gotta give action in order to get action.' This is another way to say you have to be in the game. So, go to your network members and ask for business from those who may be putting work off until later. Encourage them do it now to help you. Ask for referrals and the numbers of people who may need your products or service so you can follow up.

This is the time to be more proactive and shake the trees more vigorously. For many of us, me included, business is slow. We have to wake up and take action and figure a way out of this slowdown in our country. When you help yourself, others will follow.

I want us all to make more calls, send more emails, talk to more people, ask for more help and help others wherever and whenever you can.

Key Takeaways

1. Look at the context of any situation you perceive as a 'setback'
2. Find the positive points, not just the negative to form your perception
3. Stay focused don't let setbacks get you off track
4. Regroup and be proactive. Give action to get action in return

Failure is Not an Option

'Failure is not an Option.' I love that expression. But let's give it some context. That expression denotes an urgency of a critical moment. In business as in life, our journey is long and is a form that takes shape from the actions you take every day.

Are legendary sports player scoring every time? Tiger Woods is a fantastic golfer, but he has perfected his game through failures not wins. Winning are the trophies you pick up along the way. Failures (in order of magnitude) are what make victory so sweet. All truly successful people have said (in some form) that success is attitude combined with talent that is ready for opportunity.

J.K. Rowling is arguably one of the most overnight success authors with her mega series - Harry Potter. But she talks more about her failures and less of her successes.

"You might never fail on the scale I did," Rowling told that privileged audience. "But it is impossible to live without failing at something, unless you live so cautiously that you might as well not have lived at all—in which case, you fail by default.

Failure and Success are necessarily connected. You can't really succeed at anything without failing. If that were possible, you would have to admit you were never really challenged to succeed in the first place and someone else just handed it to you. Natural winners have skills that others may have to work hard at acquiring, but we all have our hidden talents. It is that longer-term initiative to find your talents and grow them through trial and error. Like failures, successes are intermittent.

As we look back over the past year, many of us may feel we did not do as well as we had hoped we would. In the future, people will write about the great recession of 2008-2012 and how it affected the world. Our current economic times are unlike any in recent history. To me, that means opportunity. It is time to prove what we can do by working a little harder, meeting a few more people, sending out a few more emails to contact a few more prospects. Believe in yourself and do it – Success is an attitude. Channel your talents and find opportunities for success. If your customers are happy with your product or service, they will likely be happy to refer you to their friends and clients.

This may sound like the ramblings of an optimist, but we are all struggling. I, too, am feeling the effects of the economic crisis. So what should I do? Give up? No. I work harder and smarter. I analyze what worked in the past. If it worked then, I repeat the process.

Many find it hard to be positive in times when the economy is down. People are being laid off, bank accounts are decreasing and uncertainty is rampant. I, myself, have times when I question my path and where it will lead me. It's times like these when we should reach out to those who we know and trust for help—especially in business.

My father had a saying that he lived by, "When it comes to feeding your family, failure is not an option." So with that in mind, I expect myself to be more proactive. I have to create my own stimulus package. Next time someone asks how things are going, be honest. If you need help, let them know how they can help you and be willing to do the same in return.

Top 5 Things to Remember about Success

1. Successes are intermittent milestones, but we must live a successful mindset every day.
2. The most successful people had their fair share of failures – they just don't celebrate them
3. Time invested allows opportunity for success; you have to be in the game to win. Persistence keeps you in the endurance race we call success.
4. There are critical moments where your focus can drastically determine your future – like pulling the cord on a parachute – so when you jump, be ready to pull the cord.

5. Success is nothing more and nothing less than an attitude / daily approach combined with opportunities to channel your talents.

Looking Back to See Ahead

Do you remember the saying "April showers bring May flowers?" The things we do, our efforts and actions during one month influence the activity of the future months. Our efforts are like planting seeds. Having plenty of flowers to pick later depends on how many seeds you plant now. I like that approach.

Our less flowery readers may appreciate the more direct expression "ya'gotta' give action to get action." Yet not all action has the same return on effort or ROE.

We should all do a quick analysis of our history, every so often, to see what activities we've performed over the previous five or six months that may have or may not have yielded the results we need. If your efforts are moving you forward toward your goals, then your return on your efforts and actions is paying off. Duplicate and multiply these efforts. If not, why not? What can you do better to get the results you desire? The more you try, the better you will get at discovering what is working.

Some liken the fast yet relentless action of business to that of battle – a blinding and extended well-planned initiative achieving tangible goals. There certainly is merit to this analogy but all success is had by striking a balance of activity and reflection. For all you battle reference freaks – let's call it a 'situation report' affectionately acronymed 'SITREP.' The point is - we must balance action and reflections to make sure we do not miss opportunities to change our future for the better. Measure what you do so you too can grow a beautiful flower garden with positive activity. When things are going good, make notes in a notebook or journal about your achievements.

Have you ever had to take a step back and reflect? Where am I now? Of course, we all do this from time to time. Many times it happens following a failure or misstep and sometimes after a big success. Whatever the reason, we reflect. In this time of reflection, hopefully we see ways we can improve or do things differently. What have I done wrong, and how can I avoid repeating those words or actions? What did I do right and how can I duplicate it?

It may be time for a long weekend or a vacation so you can reflect. I sometimes feel that I can slack off, if I've been doing well. This isn't true. Really, I need to ramp up and capitalize on my success so I can keep building. When you are on a roll, don't stop.

What actions are going to give you the best return on your effort or ROE? Commit to network more, sell more, refer more and help people more. I believe the key to getting on top and staying on top is to find ways to step up your game.

Commit to a Networking Blitz

I knew networking was a strength of mine, so when I bought my company and needed to grow my customer base, I set out to do a networking blitz in my areas. I went to no fewer than 5 and up to 10 networking events a week for at least 6 months. So how can you find 5 to 10 networking events per week?

What I did was join multiple networking organizations at once. I joined five local Chambers of Commerce organizations, the Women's Referral Network and the Professional Referral Exchange, a weekly networking referral group. From those groups, I found multiple events to go to weekly and I did.

In that six months I got to know many people and more importantly, many people got to know me. Many people would ask me how I went to all these events and I would just tell them, it was my job to get out and meet people. By the end of 2006, I was well known as a very active networker. I think I accomplished my goal in getting to be known. In that 6 month period, my monthly business grew by about 50% from when I started

As I said earlier, I enjoy networking and maintain a very full calendar of events for myself. I always sit down in the beginning of the month and identify the events of each organization that I need to attend and I populate my calendar accordingly. This is a way for me to try to hit each organization at least once a month.

I do this so people get used to seeing me, recognize me, get to know me, think of me when they had a computer issue and eventually hire me. I'd go to so many events that people who see me out at one or two events a month say, "Man, you are everywhere" or "you are the networking guy."

I liked that, identified with that and decided that was something good to be known for. I made it a point to get to know people and try to connect people to each other. With a growing collection of business cards, I stay organized so I know who is who and where I met them before. Like a business matchmaker. It helped me to be a good connection to others and made me memorable as a good networker.

Being everywhere and being visible is important. Finding networking events is the easy part, once you know where to look. The challenge is to find events that have the highest potential to lead to new business. Many events have fees associated with them, so networking is an investment of time and money. The conversion process from new business lead to new business sales is critical. In this book I talk about the importance of follow-up.

Key Recommendations

1. Build and commit yourself to a schedule of networking opportunities.
2. Connect with people; build relationships; be everywhere you possibly can.
3. Organize your growing collection of business cards. Mark down where you met, when, and any other relevant conversation details.
4. Follow-up where appropriate. There is a window of relevancy, where even if someone said to call them, they will lose the context and interest as time passes. Strike while the iron is hot.

Make An Ally By Being An Ally

Partnering with others can increase your business as well as theirs. Finding someone to share contacts and network with will mutually benefit both of you. This will provide each of you with a way to reach your sales goals without "cold calling." Let's look at how this can work.

Find a few people who are beneficial to you and whose business networks complement yours. These can be realtors and home inspectors, or insurance brokers and mortgage companies or computer people with copier or repair customers. These are only suggested sources. There are many fields that have customer bases that would be beneficial to tap into. Many service companies have a wealth of possible contacts.

You and your potential partner should have businesses that have a similar customer base or one with clients that have a need for the others products or services. Both parties can sit down and learn what the other person does, what their ideal customer is, and how your customers will benefit with what the other person's business can offer. Lastly, as long as your interests don't compete – meaning that you align your business goals, both parties should to commit to:

- Revealing your customers to your new partner
- Talking to your customers about your new partner
- Using your influence to help your partner meet your customers
- Sharing a number of contacts each month with that partner

Now that you have found network partners, get to know them and better identify their ideal customer. Review your list of friends and customers during your meetings and identify prospects you both can share with each other.

Set up appointments and report back after you meet the people on the list you are given. Repeat this at least once a month or more often. If you discuss your progress with your new partner, you are encouraged to voice successes or failures. With input from one another, you can improve your technique and help them do the same. By sharing referrals, both parties benefit from the networking experience. If you network with two or three people every month in this way, you will build a wide and deep pipeline of new business.

Unfortunately, however, there may be opportunities that look great when put down on paper but are not beneficial in practice. Modifications may need to be made, as the relationship becomes a work in process. It is best to be open-minded and be able to make changes when you see that it is not working.

If it does not work out, what is your exit strategy? How easy or difficult will it be to end the partnership? If it does end, can you find another partner or do you want another partner?

Many times, partnerships are great. They offer you the opportunity to grow and expand without having to add to your staff or expertise. Just make sure you go into it with proper forethought. Agree when you need to and if you see red flags, pay attention. This is a business. Keep personal feelings out of the negotiations. Make sure that "The Juice is Worth the Squeeze!"

Top Five Lessons

1. Look for opportunities to partner with others to grow each other's business.
2. Make sure the customers they have and you have can benefit each other.
3. Agree to promote each other to your networks.
4. Develop a committed strategy to work at this diligently.
5. If it does not work, either change the strategy or get out.

Using Social Networks to Expand Your Business

With the advent of online engagement, we have so many ways to multiply our efforts in networking. One of the newest and fastest growing networking tools is social networking. Are you LinkedIn? Is your face on Facebook? Are you Tweeting? This seems to be what many people are asking today. With all the different sites, which are you using, and more importantly, how do you use them for more exposure and ultimately more business?

Today, you can reach more people in the world than ever before through social networking. Let's take LinkedIn as an example. As of the writing of this book, I have over 11,000 first generation connections in LinkedIn. I am considered a super-networker at this level. In LinkedIn, you can directly communicate with your network up to three generations in. This means that I can connect with all of my 11,000 contacts and their first level contacts, which is my second level. Then I have access to their second level, which becomes my third level. So going three generations deep I have over 18,900,000 people I can connect to. In my area alone, the Philadelphia Metro Area, I have over 91,000 connections.

Establishing your social network can take a tremendous amount of time and effort. However, with some basic skills, you can significantly increase your network by adding some super-networkers to your network. Then you have access to their first and second generation, in my case that would be in excess of 3.3 million people.

Let me help you to understand the significance of this. I can market directly to my 91,000 local contacts by posting something on my LinkedIn page. I can poll this many people. I can post a workshop to this many people. I can connect either directly or by introduction to this many people. I can get some form of communication to this many people!

To enhance your knowledge of these tools, look in your local newspaper, local colleges, or go online and find books, workshops and professionals who specialize in teaching these new avenues. Spend time researching these tools. Look at what they offer and how it can help your business.

By the way, if you send me a request to connect, I will connect with you. My LinkedIn profile can be found at www.linkedin.com/in/guydunn .

Key Takeaways

1. Networking online is an essential way to reach many more people than traditional face-to-face methods
2. Online networking is global

3. Your online presence is becoming required to make you more credible to your networking connections
4. There are seemingly endless sources of information to help you build or improve your online presence – read up and stay current

Find More Time for Success

I am not always busy with my business, but I am generally busy with activities designed to move me forward. I try to see what more I can do, whether it is marketing, networking, researching and/or looking for new products and or services to offer. My normal mode of operation is to optimize my actions and squeeze as much as I can out of every day. For example, I am working on a couple of major projects that I have to devote time to without letting up on servicing my customers' needs. Time is valuable so I decided to spend more time on my business. One of my mantras is "I will sleep when I die!" In the fury of action and admittedly marginalizing the need for balance, that kind of boldness helps spur me to purpose and action by reminding me achievement requires efficient action and persistence.

Can you give another 15 minutes, 30 minutes or one more hour to your business activities? If you could add another hour to your day and could use it to make business better, what would you do? Look at how to squeeze more out of your day. Set the alarm for 30 minutes earlier or skip the 11:00 o'clock news and go to bed at 11:00p.m. The key is to find more time and then work more efficiently with that time.

Once you have found that time, maximize the outcome from reclaiming a little extra time. Fifteen minutes a day devoted to making two phone calls will reap great rewards over time. Maybe use your new found time to call on people you met at networking events. If out of those 10 calls a week, you find one or two clients, wouldn't it be worth it? If I had one additional client a week, that would be at least $12,000 additional income and more in residual income annually. That makes me want to drop this keyboard and pick up my phone right now.

We all have many things in our lives competing for priority. There is family, church, work, friends, fitness, charities, etc. In balancing who and what we devote our time to, we can all benefit by being more efficient and looking to optimize our efforts and the ultimate results.
Time is our currency for life. Use it wisely. It is the only thing that we all get in the same increments every day. My 24 hours is the same as yours, but what I do with my day is probably different from what the next person will do with theirs. You have to decide if you can get more done with the time you have. If you do more, you will accomplish more.

Top 5 Things to Remember about Time

1. We all get the same 24 hours a day; it's how we use it that differentiates us.
2. You can have more time if you adjust what you do when. Reclaim it!

3. A simple plan to use reclaimed time can yield major results over time.
4. Our life is a juggling act especially when it comes to time, choose wisely how you use it.
5. Always remember, you do have time for the things which are important, decide what is important.

Lasting Impressions

Have you ever attended a networking event, collected business cards, only to forget the person's face or your conversation after you walk away? Or try to remember someone you met and had a conversation with, but you can't remember their name or what you talked about? As soon as you step away from the person, make a short note on that person's card. By stopping for a minute to fix their face in your mind as well as noting your conversation on their card, you are committing them to memory. These memories can be a goldmine.

The same goes for their memory of you; make sure it is a goldmine for you as well. You certainly don't want to be someone people can't remember. It's all well and good to pass out business cards, but if people don't remember you, they probably won't be calling you to follow up, and they certainly won't keep you in mind for their future needs.

It is important to consider what kind of an impression you want to make. I try to make myself memorable when I meet people. It may not happen on the first meeting or the second, but after we meet a few times, I make sure I have made an impression and they will remember me.

Lasting impressions are made by staying visible and staying relevant to your target contacts. So, the strategy is to build your brand, stay connected and thus create a lasting impression.

There are a couple of easy steps for engaging people. Look people in the eyes and be present. Don't scan the room while you are talking to someone. If they are taking the time to talk with you, make the time to give them your time. Then ask them something that will allow you to remember them so when you see them the next time you can refer to it. For example, tell a quick story about something so they will have more than a handshake to remember you by. The idea is to have something out of the ordinary from a personal dynamic or content perspective so that people will remember you.

Your opening topic may just be about politics or the weather, but this is the perfect opportunity for you to become acquainted with people who you may be able to help—or who may be able to help you to expand your business. Taking advantage of times like these can spark interesting conversations as well as create contacts.

If you are giving them a business card or some type of corporate collateral, make it different, memorable, useful and or easy to use. For instance, you could create an odd sized card so it stands out from all of the other cards they get. Or you could provide content in the form of a brochure, book, or a magazine.

Be one of the few people that your new contact is likely to remember. A kind smile, during a person's busy day, can be memorable. Perhaps it is even just providing a referral. But make sure you always follow-up quickly.

Here is another networking tip. Talk to people who are in line for an event registration, or in a line for coffee, or as you wait to pay for your groceries or wait to talk to the bank teller. Introduce yourself and say something like: "We might as well make the best of our time while we are here. My name is _____, what's yours? I'm in the _____ field. What do you do?"

Someone may even overhear you and speak up or ask you a question. This would be a good place to practice your 30 second commercial and express your interests. When you are alone, make a few notes in a notebook or journal regarding the people you met and write down what you want to remember about them. Also, take some time every so often to think back in time to last year and make a list of the people you haven't seen or talked to for some time. Pick up the phone or make a note to follow up with these people.

Key Takeaways

1. Improve your networking memory skills by associating people with events or topics that are related to your introduction
2. Lasting impressions are made by staying visible and staying relevant to your target contacts

3. Practice your engagement skills – look them in the eye and share an interesting point of view

4. Leave people with your memorable contact information in the form of non-standard business cards or a relevant piece of content or collateral.

Resources to Improve Your Business

If you want to become a resource, you must amass your own critical resources. The list of resources now available online are seemingly endless. But be careful what you repurpose from the Internet to advance your own business. Just because the information is out on the Net does not mean that it's right. Gauge the content against your own sense and knowledge. Look at how new thoughts, ideas, and methodologies are really stacking up in experts' opinion.

Need more stimulating inspiration? Nothing says commitment to a cause that participation at a tradeshow. The Consumer Electronic Show (CES) in Las Vegas may provide the inspiration you need. There's also nothing quite like innovation, new products and the showcasing of products, and services to encourage growth. What inspired me the most when I attended was seeing the potential of these products and services and what they can do to create new ideas. Use this opportunity to motivate yourself and your partners.

Going to shows and conventions gives us the opportunity to see the latest and greatest in our fields. Make it a point to go to at least one industry related convention and/or trade show each year. Mingle with some of your peers from across the country and sometimes across the world. The purpose is two-fold: it enables you to keep up with technology and information about your industry to better serve your clients and network partners. Mingling with others who also do what you do and seeing how they achieve their goals will only make you more knowledgeable.

If you want to be a resource to others, find resources for yourself. Learn, grow and expand your knowledge. Find something new and exciting that you can bring to your network. Not only will it help you get excited, it will motivate you.

Key Lessons

1. If you want to become a resource, you must amass your own resources.
2. Make sure that you know subject matter to become an expert.
3. Just because information is on the Internet doesn't mean it is right or accurate – so consider your sources.
4. Continually use new sources to stay inspired an stimulated.
5. You never stop growing or learning.

Newsletter Pointers

A newsletter is great way to send out information and keep in touch with your customers and those with whom you would like to initiate a networking relationship. Take advantage of special occasions or marketing opportunities like holidays, seasons, political events, anniversaries, etc. to visit those who advertise and are the focus in articles in your newsletter.

Be relevant to your target audience by providing news that can help your clients and featuring those subjects. Find individual items of interest specific to your clients that show them that you are interested in their business. Having a newsletter can give you an excuse for visiting them and not just talking about your business. In this way, you will cultivate consistent readers of your newsletter.

Now that we have the Internet, social media at our disposal; we can put our newsletter on easy to reach channels of communication. It is much easier to update and distribute this way. Your Internet-based newsletter can include such things as monthly calendars with events of importance. Your readers will start using your newsletter as a point to regularly find the information that they need. This can only help your exposure.

Put a blog comment field at the bottom of the page so your readers can make suggestions and comments. List articles as a menu item, with past articles available for clicking and reading. Advertising will draw people to your website. Mentioning or advertising books and items from Amazon and other places will help make your site an authority to consult. Readers appreciate knowing about other eBooks and articles that are free. Your newsletter will provide your readers with sources of information and network possibilities that can only help your business grow.

You don't have to create your newsletter for just your industry. If you get off track or 'go on a personal rant', people may tolerate short indulgences but you risk becoming irrelevant and losing their continued interest. Put yourself in your audiences' shoes. Imagine what the general public may want to know. What are the events going on in your area that the average person would be interested in knowing about? Be aware of the events that are happening around where you do business. When people read your newsletter for general information, you broaden your reader base. If you chose to charge for advertising, the number of readers that you draw can have a positive impact.

You are welcome to refer to my website and read my newsletter as an example @ www.theideaguyonline.com/

Five Key Lessons on Newsletters

1. Providing relevant information to interested audiences is a great way of building a network of seekers looking for your information.
2. Take advantage of social channels that help build new connections and reaffirm existing connections.
3. Let your information consumers give you feedback.
4. Don't forget that advertising works.
5. Make sure your topics are focused and industry-related, tangents are an indulgence.

Take Time to Reflect and Assess

Remember in earlier chapters, I talked about balance and reflection? It is critical when making more time that we schedule some of that time to gauge where we are, where we are going, and what we need to change to make something happen. That knowledge will afford us the opportunity to adjust our plan and make the appropriate course corrections.

Happily, our globally shared calendar gives us a time frame and perspective to help us determine progress and work towards change. The downside to this shared timeline is that it's easy to be distracted by artificial hurdles such as missing self-imposed milestones. Milestones are just that, they mark a path on a journey. If we haven't achieved what we had hoped for during a particular period of time – maybe our goals were not realistic.

I am always one to focus on what has been accomplished and see the opportunities ahead. Sure, I could have done more in the time given, but I am an optimist and can readily show you how it could have been worse. I think that if you give yourself some goals and then you don't achieve them all, look at what you have achieved, celebrate those, and commit to do better in the future.

On the flip side, you should not be soft on yourself either. If you have been slacking off, recognize this and look closely at why you have not applied inspiration to action. Be honest with yourself-only you know the real reason(s). If you are not motivated to do more than you are doing and you are dissatisfied with your performance, then maybe you should be doing something else, like consulting with experts.

I am one who believes we should all strive to lead happy lives. That is the ultimate reward. Find what you love to do and can do well, and find a way to make a living doing it. I have been blessed, making a living at fixing computers, which began as a hobby. Through this occupation, I am able to help people, which I have a passion for, and I have the opportunity to be an entrepreneur. I am able to do something I enjoy, and I get paid for it. What's better than that?

Choose what it is that you want to do and have a passion for. To be great, you must be committed to it. Share your greatness. My daughter, who is a self-proclaimed band geek (she has been in band going on seven years now), is trying a new instrument this year, the tuba. To be great at what you want to do—not just good but great—you must train like an athlete and train not only when the group practices, but on your own time. That will make the difference between being good and being great.

Key Lessons on Reflection

1. To balance effort against performance, periods of reflection provide necessary time for self-assessment and should lead to course-corrections.
2. We have the same number of hours in a day and the same days in a year – how are your measuring your efforts?
3. Honest self-assessment is vital to future progress.
4. Do what you do well but remember that happiness is the ultimate reward.
5. Be passionate about whatever you endeavor to do – become an expert and share with others.

Success And All Its Meanings

Why do we work? Some work to earn a living, some work to add value by giving back – many people do both. These become relevant starting points when you consider what success really means to you. How do you measure success? Some measure it in monetary terms or with a job title; some by how many things they have and still others by how well their business is doing. We all have our own definition of success.

You have heard the expression – what would you do for $1 million? That is a challenge expression to find out how far you would go or how much you would do. It's a silly question though, we all want money to meet our needs. Need and success are relative to our perspective. Check out the guy in the $500k Porsche and then look at a parent watching their child hit a home run in a little-league game. The look of satisfaction is comparable.

I personally believe success is a balance of spiritual awareness, family, finances, friends and fitness. The issue is that we have a balancing act to perform every day. Sometimes we get thrown off by one thing or another. For instance, I plan appointments with clients and a family member calls to say they have a problem or need help. I may have to reschedule with my client.

These are times when I have to weigh the priorities in my life. Being able to think on your feet without getting flustered and handling issues quickly is a sign of success. Juggling life and making it work for ourselves is a bi-product of success. Some do it better than others do.

Periodically, we each need to step back and reevaluate the juggling act we perform and where we need to adjust and make improvements. We have to look at the priorities in our lives and decide which ones are most important. Success is a good thing but we have to keep it in perspective with the rest of our life. When necessary, find ways to delegate tasks and/or shift those areas that are out of balance. It takes practice.

This includes your networking activities too. Balance it out with the rest of your life; add it as an important aspect and figure out how much of a slice of your life it needs to take. You have to decide what works for you. My hope is that your life will have balance and your personal idea of success will be achieved.

Key Takeaways

1. Success is relative to how you define it for yourself.
2. Achieving your success goals will make you happy only if they are true to who you are and what you value.
3. If cash is your only goal you may find yourself rich and empty.

4. Balancing priorities means that we have set some limits and we must evaluate those every day.

Reflecting and Recap

Where did last year go? Since our journey is never over, we need to always look ahead and plan for the future while we assess the past, and the lessons learned, to help avoid setbacks.

Be optimistic. Look at the future in a positive light. We all need a tool box of "things that work" that we can turn to. Your tools are your network of contacts. Decide how to best utilize your contacts as you move forward. Ask yourself, "Who can I help now and in the future?" I make an ally by being an ally.

Ask: "What can I do in my business to move it forward?" Enhance your social media, your website, products and/or services. "What more can I do to help my customers (which, of course, will help me)?" This is just me and what I do. How about you? I hope you use this opportunity, a new year, to think about the what, where, why and how of your life. Hopefully, one year from now you can look back and smile at what you have accomplished.

~ *The End* ~

Post Note: Putting your opinion out there is always an interesting experience! I welcome any and all of your comments. Please email me @ **guysnetworknews@gmail.com** .

Sources of Inspiration

The following authors and books have helped to guide and inspire me.

Awaken the Giant Within : How to Take Immediate Control of Your Mental, Emotional, Physical and Financial Destiny! **by Anthony Robbins**

Goals!: How to Get Everything You Want -- Faster Than You Ever Thought Possible **by Brian Tracy**

Success Starts With Attitude **, by James Malinchak**

Reposition Yourself: Living Life Without Limits **by T.D. Jakes**

The Go-Giver: A Little Story About a Powerful Business Idea **by Bob Burg and John David Mann**

No B.S.Trust-Based Marketing: The Ultimate Guide to Creating Trust in an Understandably UN-Trusting World **by Dan S. Kennedy, Matt Zagula**

Little Gold Book of YES! Attitude: How to Find, Build and Keep a YES! Attitude for a Lifetime of SUCCESS by **Jeffrey H. Gitomer**

Empower and Equip Others!
Share this Book

Networking For Business Contacts + Opportunity = Success
It's not just who you know, It's what you do once you know them!

Wouldn't it be great to have a manual to help you understand and execute your networking activities. One that lays it out so you develop a plan to win every time? Give your networking activities a boost. Make sure you are armed with the knowledge to make every event count. These tips and stories are easy to read, understand and implement. So share it with network!

Special Quantity Discounts

2-20	Books	$ 8.50
21-99	Books	$7.50
100-499	Books	$7.00
500 +	Books	$6.00

To Place Order Call 215-680-9192